SOUTH HOLLAND PUBLIC LIBRARY

3 1350 00214 4964

P9-DHB-019

South Holland Public Library
South Holland, Illinois

Word Bird's

Christmas Words

Published in the United States of America by The Child's World®, Inc.
PO Box 326
Chanhassen, MN 55317-0326
800-599-READ
www.childsworld.com

Project Manager Mary Berendes
Editor Katherine Stevenson, Ph.D.
Designer Ian Butterworth

Copyright © 2002 by The Child's World®, Inc.
All rights reserved. No part of this book may be
reproduced or utilized in any form or by any means
without written permission from the publisher.

Library of Congress Cataloging-in-Publication Data
Moncure, Jane Belk.
Word Bird's Christmas words / by Jane Belk Moncure.
p. cm.
Summary: Word Bird puts words about Christmas in his word house—
North Pole, reindeer, candy canes, stockings, and others.
ISBN 1-56766-625-6 (lib. bdg. : alk. paper)
1. Vocabulary—Juvenile literature.
2. Christmas—Juvenile literature. [1. Vocabulary. 2. Christmas. 3. Holidays.] I. Title.
PE1449 .M527 2001
428.1—dc21
00-010897

DISCARD
3 1350 00214 4964

Word Bird's

Christmas Words

by Jane Belk Moncure

illustrated by Chris McEwan

DISCARD

SOUTH HOLLAND PUBLIC LIBRARY

Word Bird made a...

word house.

"I will put Christmas
words in my house,"
said Word Bird.

Word Bird put in these words:

Dear Santa,

I have been a very good bird.

Santa Claus
North Pole

letter

North Pole

Santa's workshop

elves

reindeer

sleigh

Santa Claus

Christmas trees

balls

stars

candles

carolers

jingle bells

Christmas cookies

candy canes

toy store

wrappings

gifts

Christmas cards

mistletoe

poinsettias

holly

Christmas flowers

stockings

Christmas story

silent night

Merry Christmas

Can you read these Christmas

letter

Santa Claus

North Pole

Christmas trees

Santa's workshop

balls

stars

elves

candles

reindeer

carolers

sleigh

jingle bells

words with Word Bird?

Christmas cookies

Christmas flowers

candy canes

stockings

toy store

Christmas story

wrappings

silent night

gifts

Christmas cards

Merry Christmas

You can make a Christmas word house. You can put Word Bird's words in your house and read them, too.

Can you think of other Christmas words to put in your word house?